BRAIN QUEST

LEARN to WRITE

LETTERS

T0010761

workman
· New York ·

This book belongs to:

First Name

Last Name

Copyright © 2023 by Workman Publishing, a subsidiary of Hachette Book Group, Inc.

All rights reserved. No portion of this book may be reproduced—mechanically, electronically, or by any other means, including photocopying—without written permission of the publisher.

ISBN 978-1-5235-1600-1

Design by Daniella Graner and John Passineau
Illustrations by Tiago Americo
Edited by Alisha Zucker

Workman books are available at special discounts when purchased in bulk for premiums and sales promotions as well as for fundraising or educational use. Special editions or book excerpts can also be created to specification. For details, please contact special.markets@hbgusa.com.

Workman Publishing Co., Inc., a subsidiary of Hachette Book Group, Inc.
1290 Avenue of the Americas
New York, NY 10104

workman.com

Distributed in Europe by Hachette Livre, 58 rue Jean Bleuzen, 92 178 Vanves Cedex, France.

Distributed in the United Kingdom by Hachette Book Group, UK, Carmelite House, 50 Victoria Embankment, London EC4Y 0DZ.

WORKMAN, BRAIN QUEST, and IT'S FUN TO BE SMART! are registered trademarks of Workman Publishing Co., Inc., a subsidiary of Hachette Book Group, Inc.

Printed in Canada on responsibly sourced paper.

First printing July 2023

10 9 8 7 6 5 4 3 2 1

DEAR PARENTS AND CAREGIVERS,

At Brain Quest we believe learning is an adventure, a quest for knowledge. We're delighted to partner with you and your child as they begin their exciting journey exploring the fundamentals of writing.

LEARN TO WRITE: LETTERS provides lots of opportunities for your child to write their ABCs. They'll practice writing upper and lowercase letters, learning beginning and ending sounds, and writing simple words. These skills build a foundation for writing and phonics, and they set your child up for future reading success.

Tips for Using This Book:

Follow your child's lead. Let them decide how much writing to do in one sitting.

Be hands on. Guide your child to trace the large blue letters with their fingers and the light blue letters with their pencils.

Offer support. Read the directions aloud or model how to hold the pencil correctly as needed.

Praise their effort. Compliment your learner's effort and persistence.

Celebrate success! Use stickers from the back of the book to reward effort and success, and cut out the certificate to mark your child's accomplishment.

Enjoy this first step as your child learns to write!

—The editors of Brain Quest

Hold the pencil with the thumb and index fingers. Rest the pencil on the middle finger.

4

Ants

Trace the capital letter **A**.

Write the letter **A**. Start at the **red** dot.

Trace the **A**s.

Aunt Ana

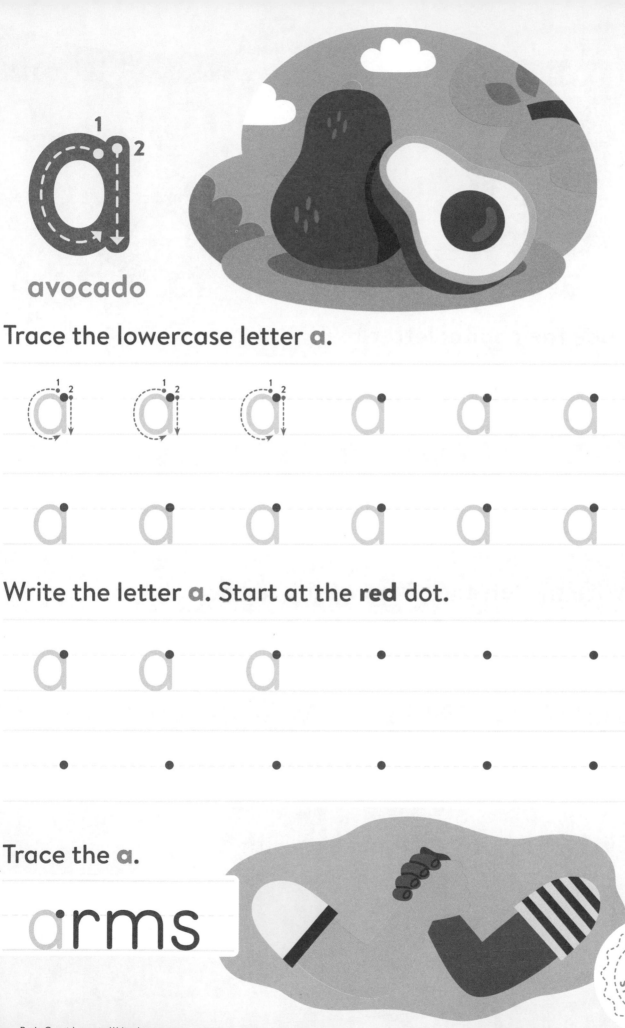

a

avocado

Trace the lowercase letter a.

Write the letter a. Start at the red dot.

Trace the a.

arms

PLACE STICKER HERE

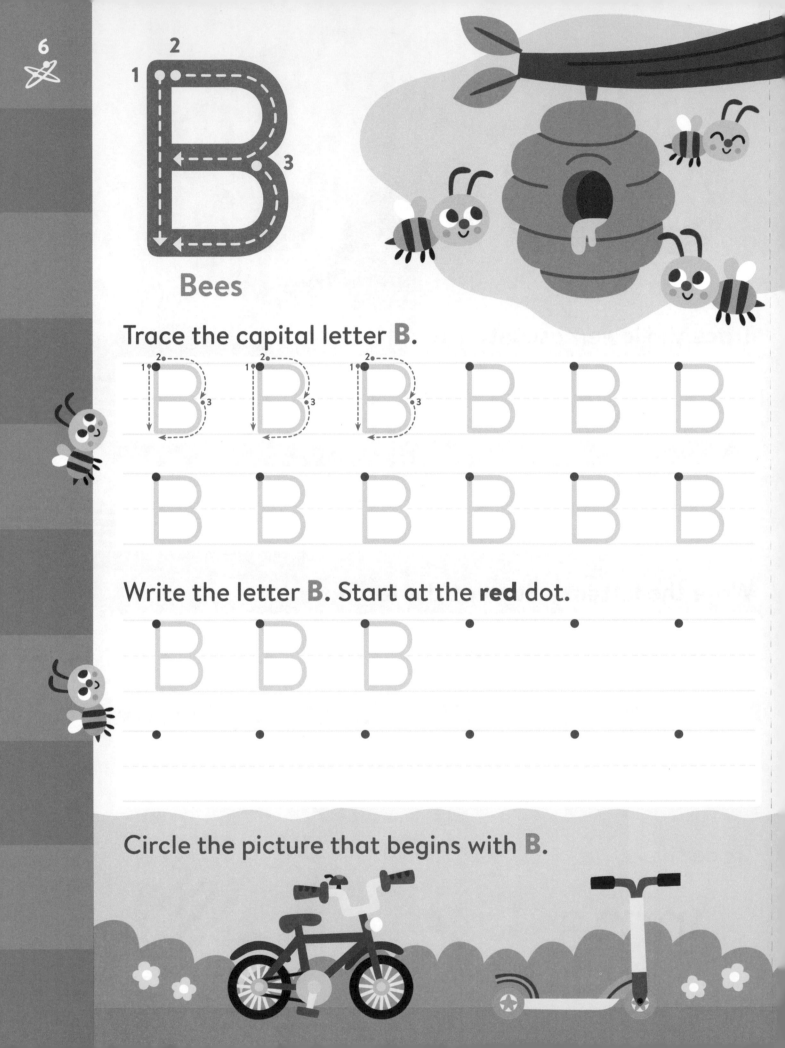

B

Bees

Trace the capital letter B.

Write the letter B. Start at the red dot.

Circle the picture that begins with B.

b

blueberries

Trace the lowercase letter b.

b b b b b b

b b b b b b

Write the letter b. Start at the red dot.

b b b

Trace the bs.

bubbles

PLACE STICKER HERE

C ¹

Cats

Trace the capital letter C.

C C C C C C C

C C C C C C

Write the letter C. Start at the red dot.

C C C

Trace the Cs to complete each word.

Cute Cow

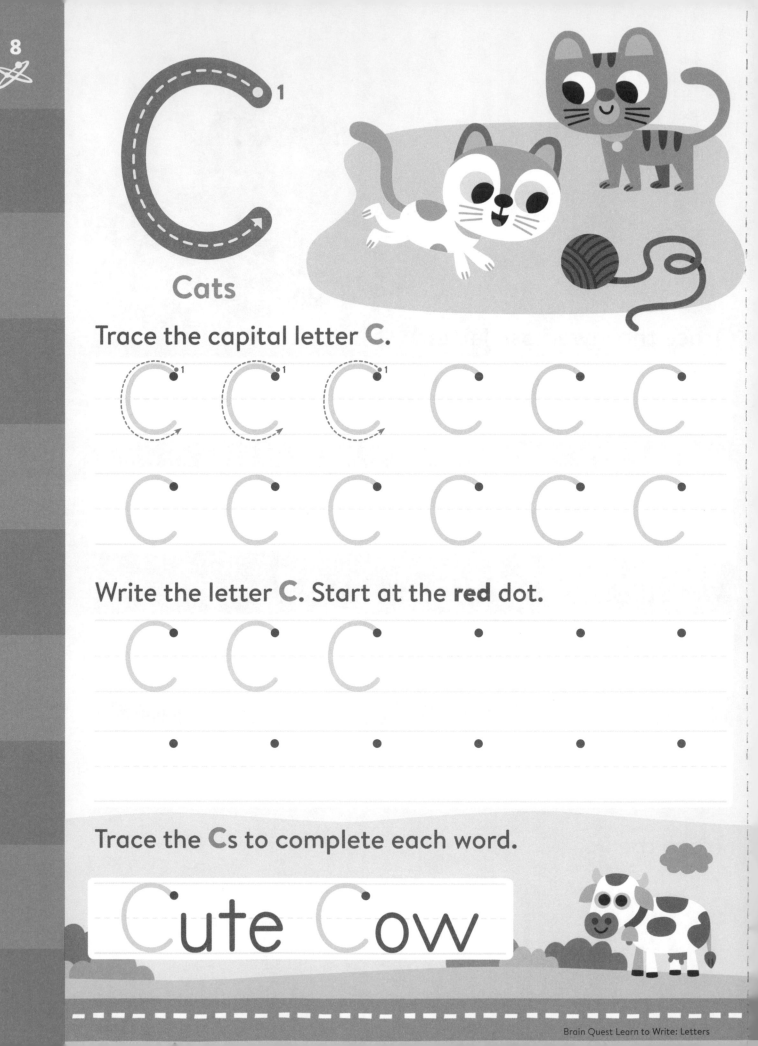

C¹
cookies

Trace the lowercase letter **c**.

c c c c c c

c c c c c c

Write the letter **c**. Start at the **red** dot.

c c c • • •

• • • • • •

Circle the **c**s.

c
a
b   a   b
c   b   c

1 2
D

Dogs

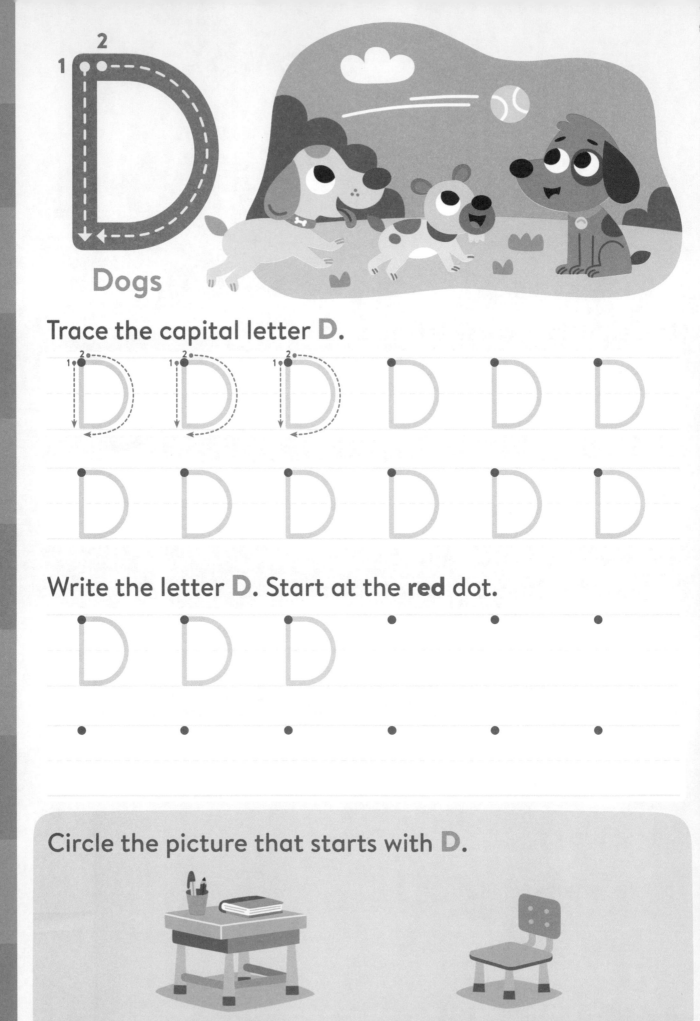

Trace the capital letter **D**.

Write the letter **D**. Start at the **red** dot.

Circle the picture that starts with **D**.

d

dinosaur

Trace the lowercase letter d.

d d d d d d

d d d d d d

Write the letter d. Start at the **red** dot.

d d d

Trace the d.

dancer

PLACE STICKER HERE

E

Eggs

Trace the capital letter E.

Write the letter E. Start at the **red** dot.

Trace the E.

Earth

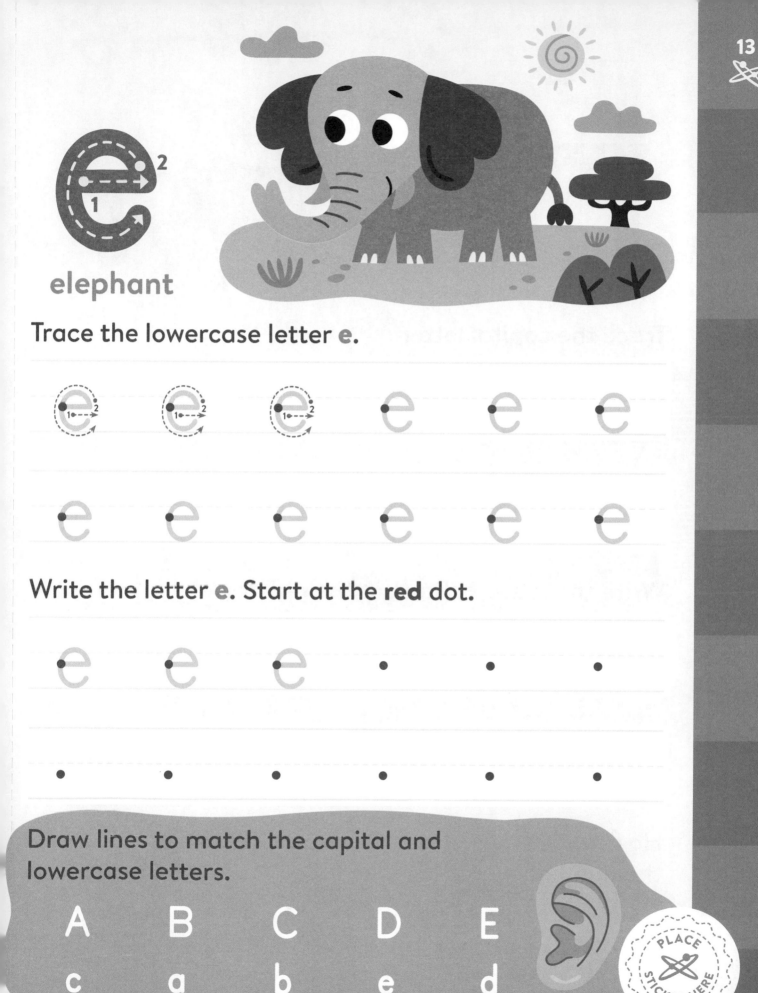

elephant

Trace the lowercase letter **e**.

Write the letter **e**. Start at the **red** dot.

Draw lines to match the capital and lowercase letters.

A   B   C   D   E

c   a   b   e   d

PLACE STICKER HERE

F

Frog

Trace the capital letter F.

Write the letter F. Start at the red dot.

How many frogs? Trace the F to write the number.

Five

f

fish

Trace the lowercase letter **f**.

f f f f f f

f f f f f f

Write the letter **f**. Start at the **red** dot.

f f f

Circle the **f**s.

e f e

f d d f d

PLACE STICKER HERE

Geese

Trace the capital letter **G**.

Write the letter **G**. Start at the **red** dot.

Trace the **G**.

Mother Goose

g gifts

Trace the lowercase letter g.

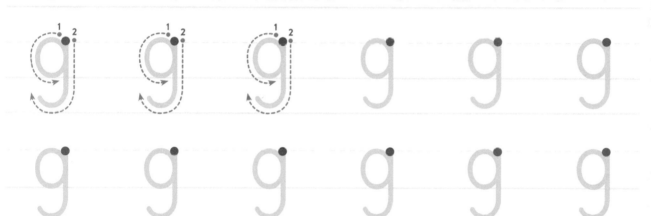

Write the letter g.
Start at the **red** dot.

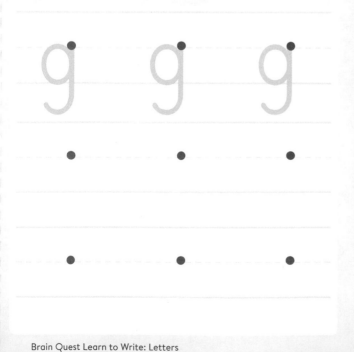

Circle the fruit that starts with g.

PLACE STICKER HERE

Let's Review

Trace the letters to complete the labels.

dog

cat

ants

H

Hippo

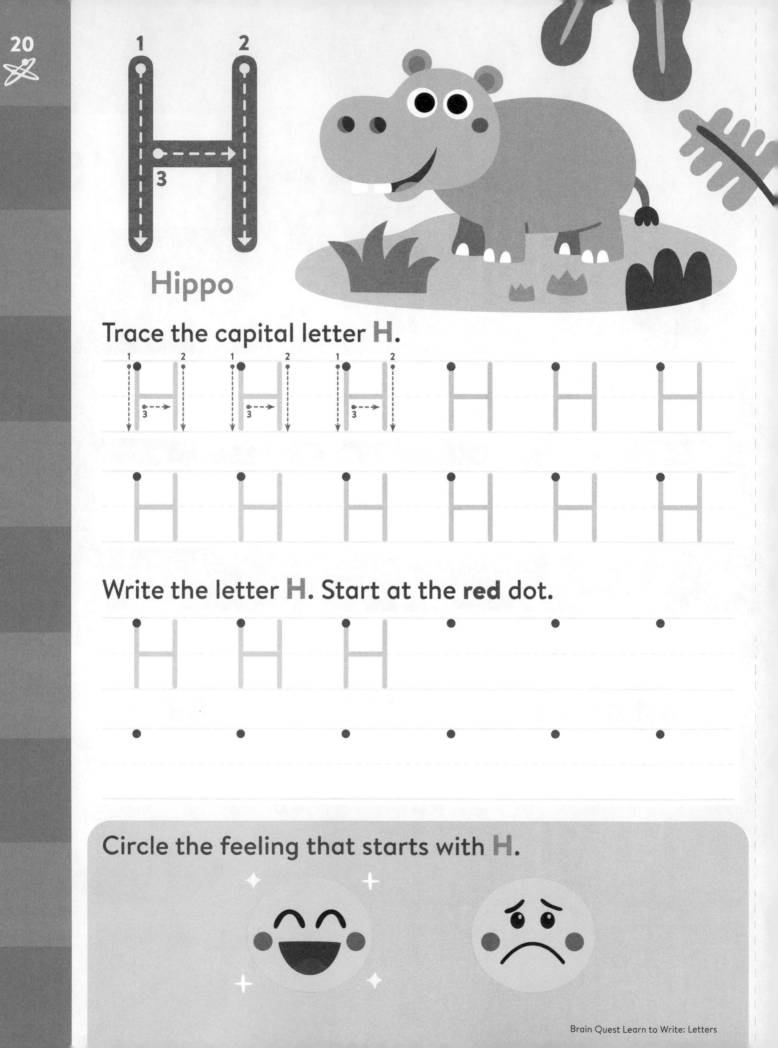

Trace the capital letter H.

Write the letter H. Start at the red dot.

Circle the feeling that starts with H.

h
hats

Trace the lowercase letter **h**.

Write the letter **h**. Start at the **red** dot.

Trace the **h** in each word.

hen

hog

PLACE STICKER HERE

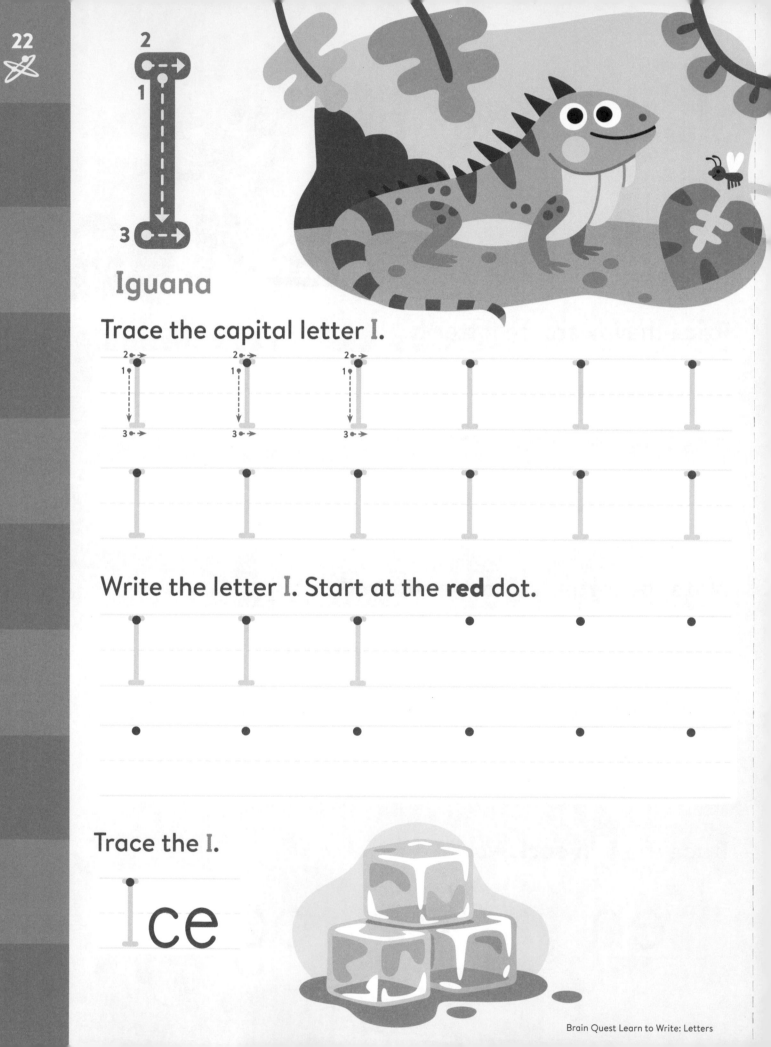

Iguana

Trace the capital letter I.

Write the letter I. Start at the **red** dot.

Trace the I.

Ice

i

island

Trace the lowercase letter i.

Write the letter i. Start at the **red** dot.

Draw lines to match the capital and lowercase letters.

A   C   G   I

c   a   i   g

J

Jaguar

Trace the capital letter J.

J J J J J J

J J J J J J

Write the letter J. Start at the **red** dot.

J J J

Circle the Js.

H H J
J
I H
J I
J H

j jump

Trace the lowercase letter j.

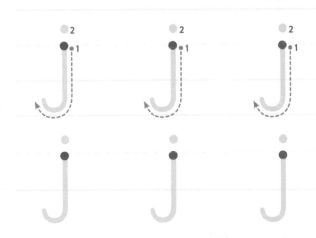

Write the letter j.
Start at the **red** dot.

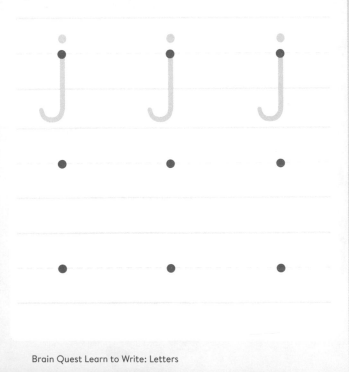

Circle the food that starts with j.

K

Kangaroo

Trace the capital letter K.

Write the letter K. Start at the red dot.

Trace the Ks to complete the name.

King Kai

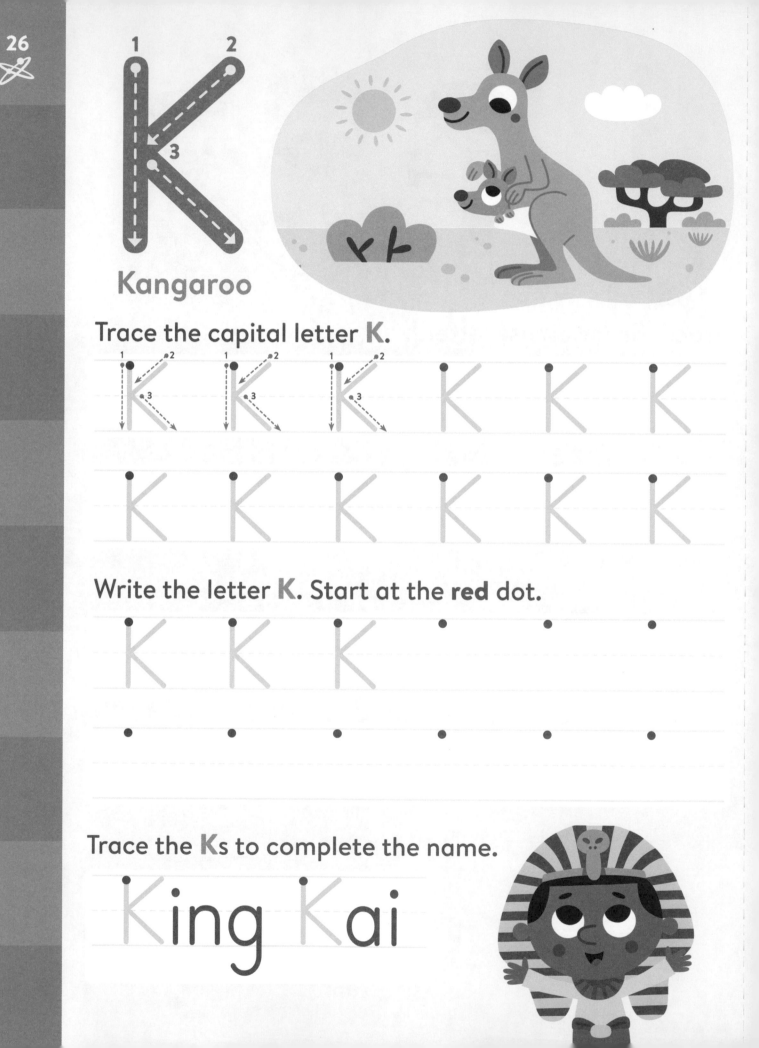

k

kids

Trace the lowercase letter k.

k k k k k k

k k k k k k

Write the letter k. Start at the **red** dot.

k k k

Write the missing k.

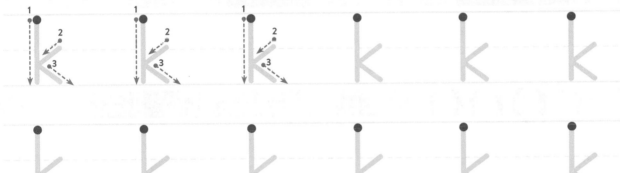

●oala

PLACE STICKER HERE

Let's Review

Trace the letters to complete the labels.

Iguana

Hippo

Jaguar

Koala

Trace the first letter and say its sound out loud.
Draw a line to match the words to the pictures.

Kayak

Jet

Bus

Cab

Dirt bike

Fire truck

Lion

Trace the capital letter L.

Write the letter L. Start at the **red** dot.

Circle the picture that starts with L.

1

love

Trace the lowercase letter **l**.

Write the letter **l**. Start at the **red** dot.

Trace the **l**.

lionfish

PLACE STICKER HERE

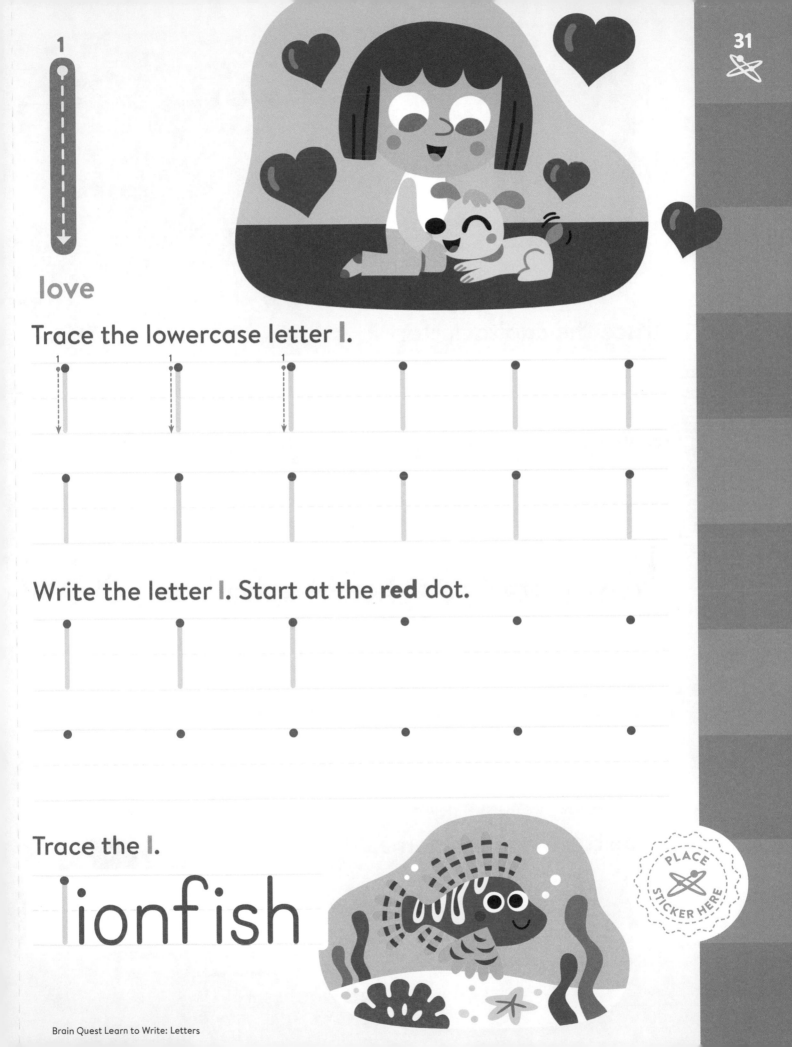

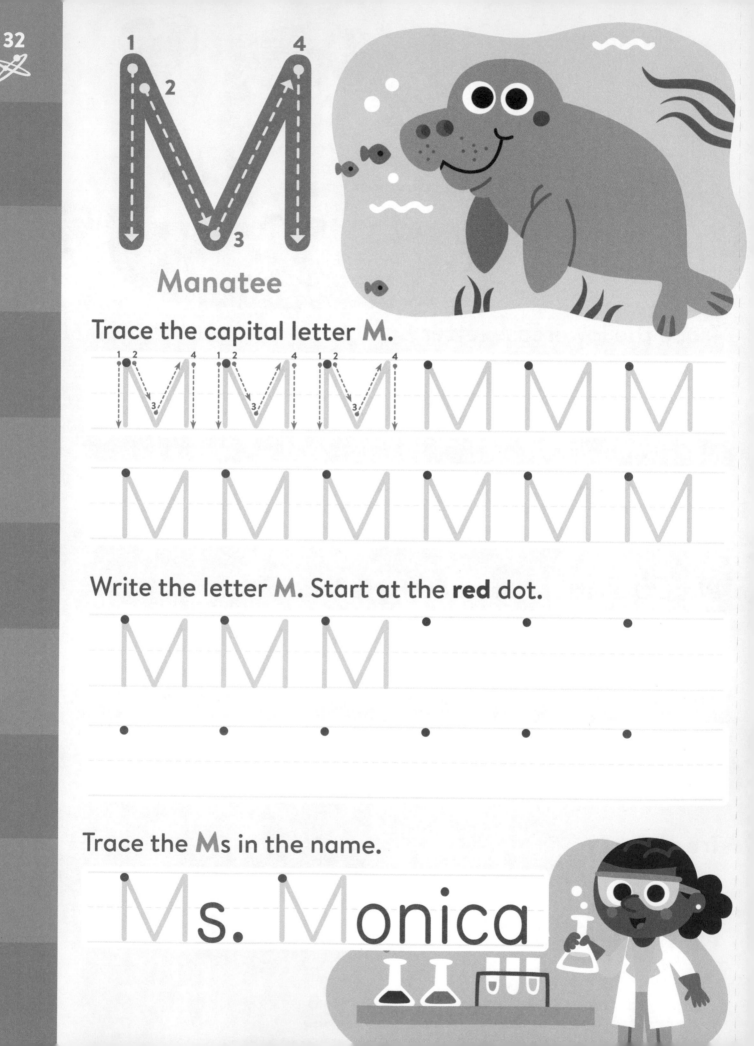

Manatee

Trace the capital letter **M**.

Write the letter **M**. Start at the **red** dot.

Trace the **M**s in the name.

Ms. Monica

m

map

Trace the lowercase letter **m**.

m m m m m m

m m m m m m

Write the letter **m**. Start at the **red** dot.

m m m

Write the missing **m**.

_oon

PLACE STICKER HERE

N

Narwhal

Trace the capital letter N.

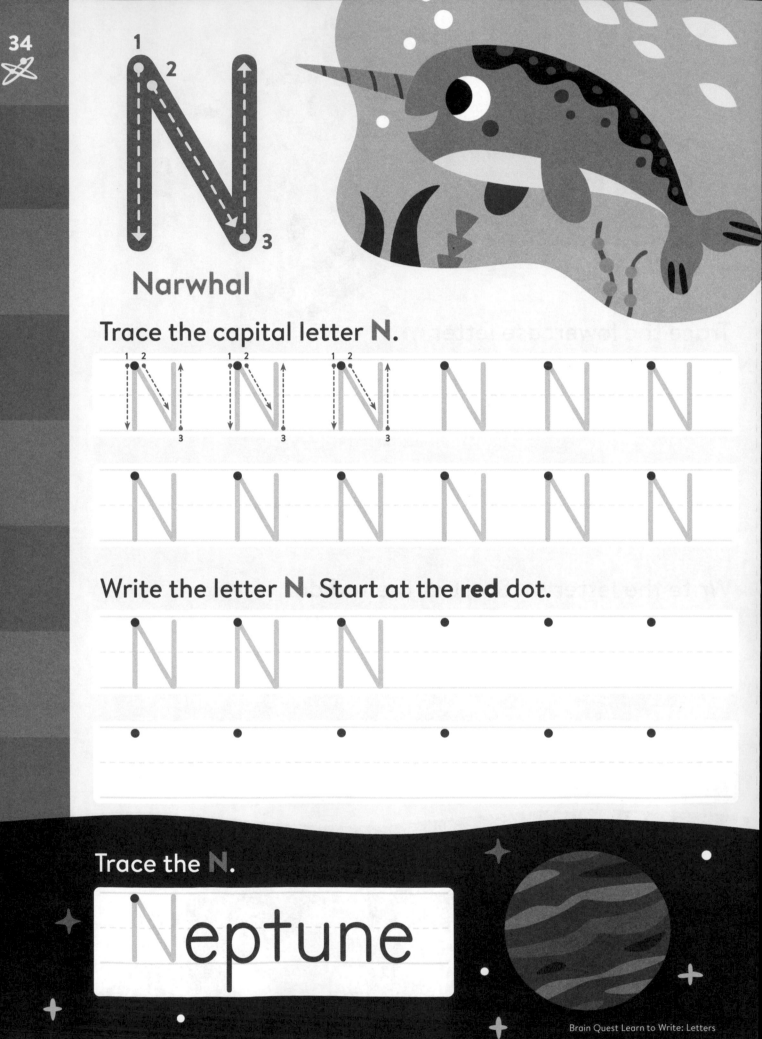

Write the letter N. Start at the red dot.

Trace the N.

Neptune

n

nose

Trace the lowercase letter n.

Write the letter n. Start at the red dot.

Circle the ns.

a	n	m	n
m	a	n	m
n	n	m	a

PLACE STICKER HERE

1

Octopus

Trace the capital letter **O**.

Write the letter **O**. Start at the **red** dot.

Circle the animal that starts with **O**.

1

onion

Trace the lowercase letter o.

Write the letter o. Start at the **red** dot.

Trace the os.

oboe

PLACE STICKER HERE

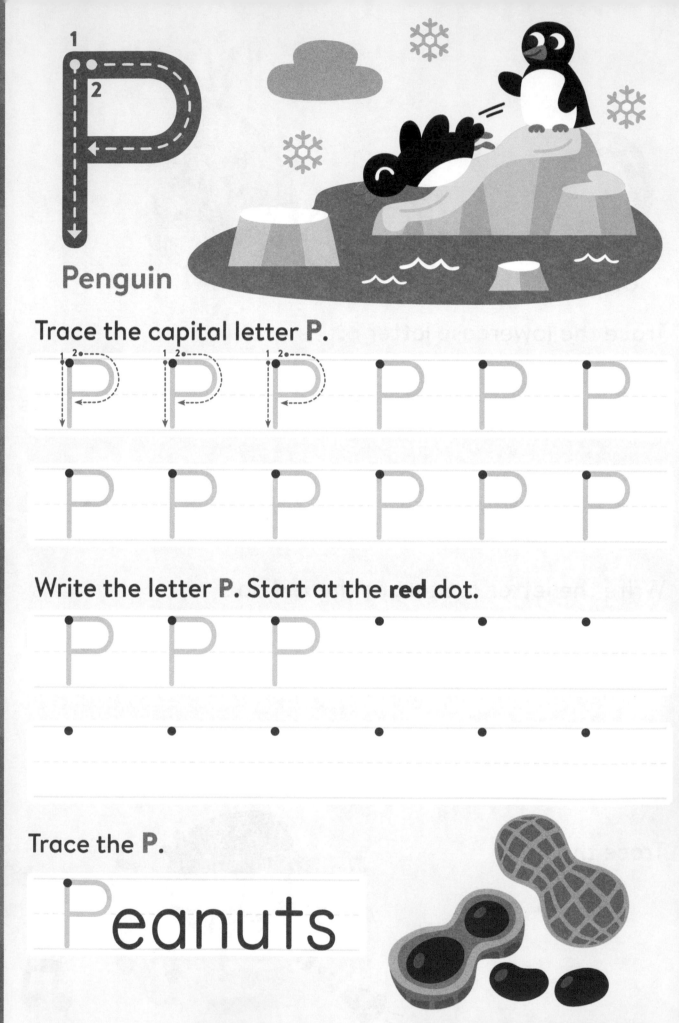

P

Penguin

Trace the capital letter P.

Write the letter P. Start at the red dot.

Trace the P.

Peanuts

p **pool**

Trace the lowercase letter **p.**

p p p p p p

p p p p p p

Write the letter **p.** Start at the **red** dot.

p p p · · ·

· · · · · ·

Write the missing **p.**

· ond

Let's Review

Trace the letters to complete the labels.

Penguin

Narwhal

Manatee

Lionfish

Octopus

Queen

Trace the capital letter Q.

Write the letter Q. Start at the **red** dot.

Trace the Q.

Quetzal

quiet

Trace the lowercase letter q.

Write the letter q. Start at the red dot.

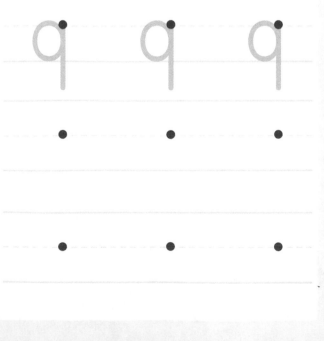

Write the missing q.

·uilt

PLACE STICKER HERE

R

Raccoon

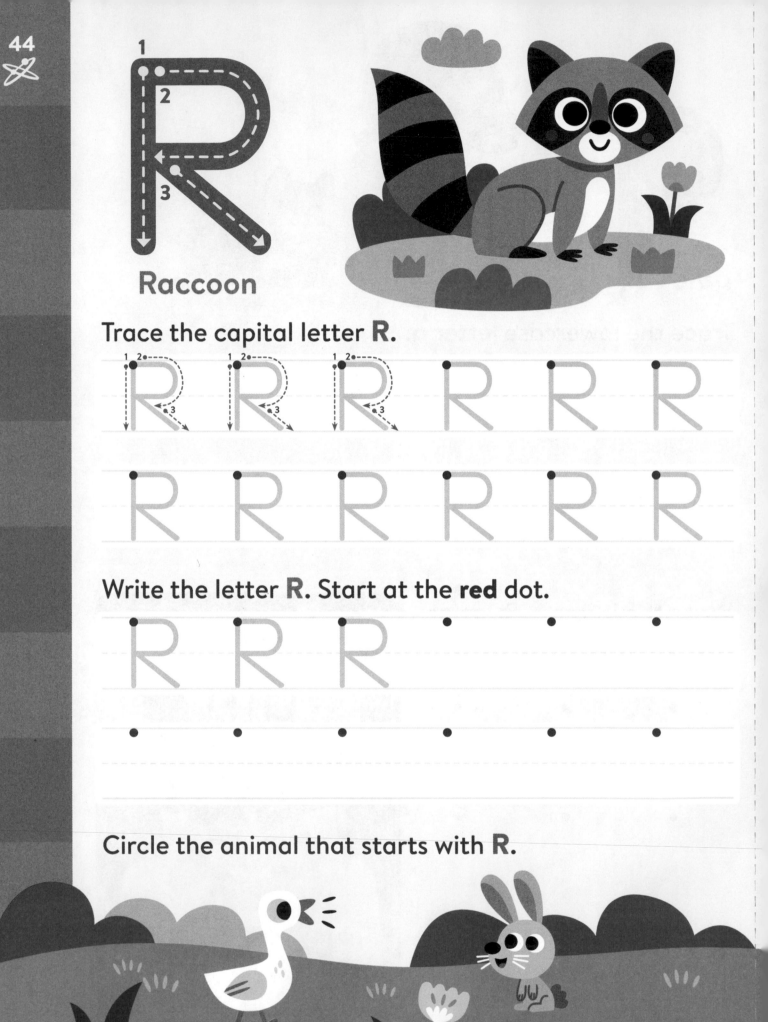

Trace the capital letter **R**.

Write the letter **R**. Start at the **red** dot.

Circle the animal that starts with **R**.

radish

Trace the lowercase letter r.

r r r r r r

r r r r r r

Write the letter r. Start at the red dot.

r r r • • •

• • • • • •

Circle the rs.

a r o n a

n a r o

r o n a r

PLACE STICKER HERE

Stork

Trace the capital letter **S**.

Write the letter **S**. Start at the **red** dot.

Trace each **S** to complete the name.

Sir Sam

s [1]

sun

Trace the lowercase letter **s**.

s s s s s s

s s s s s s

Write the letter **s**. Start at the **red** dot.

s s s • • •

• • • • • •

Write each missing **s**.

·eal

·ock

PLACE STICKER HERE

Toucan

Trace the capital letter **T**.

Write the letter **T**. Start at the **red** dot.

Circle each **T**.

R P T R P T
I P I P R P
R T I

turtle

Trace the lowercase letter t.

Write the letter t. Start at the **red** dot.

Circle the pictures that start with t.

PLACE STICKER HERE

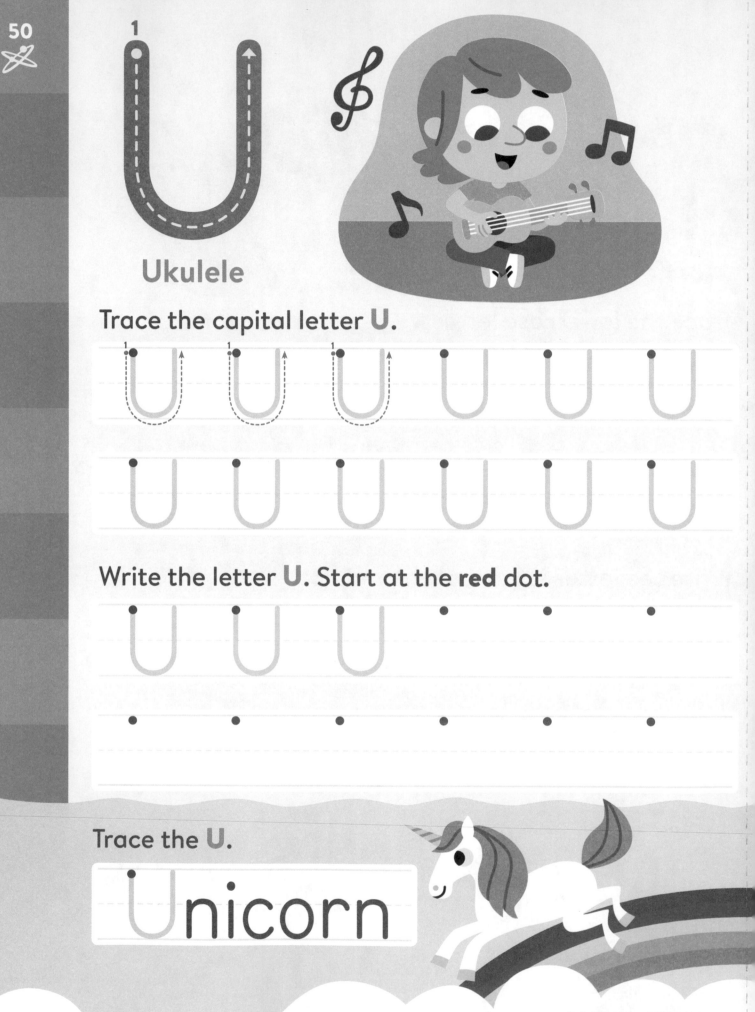

Ukulele

Trace the capital letter **U**.

Write the letter **U**. Start at the **red** dot.

Trace the **U**.

Unicorn

u
umbrella

Trace the lowercase letter **u**.

u u u u u u

u u u u u u

Write the letter **u**. Start at the **red** dot.

u u u

Circle each **u**.

n a u
u c u n a
a n c u c

V

Violin

Trace the capital letter V.

Write the letter V. Start at the red dot.

Circle the pictures that start with V.

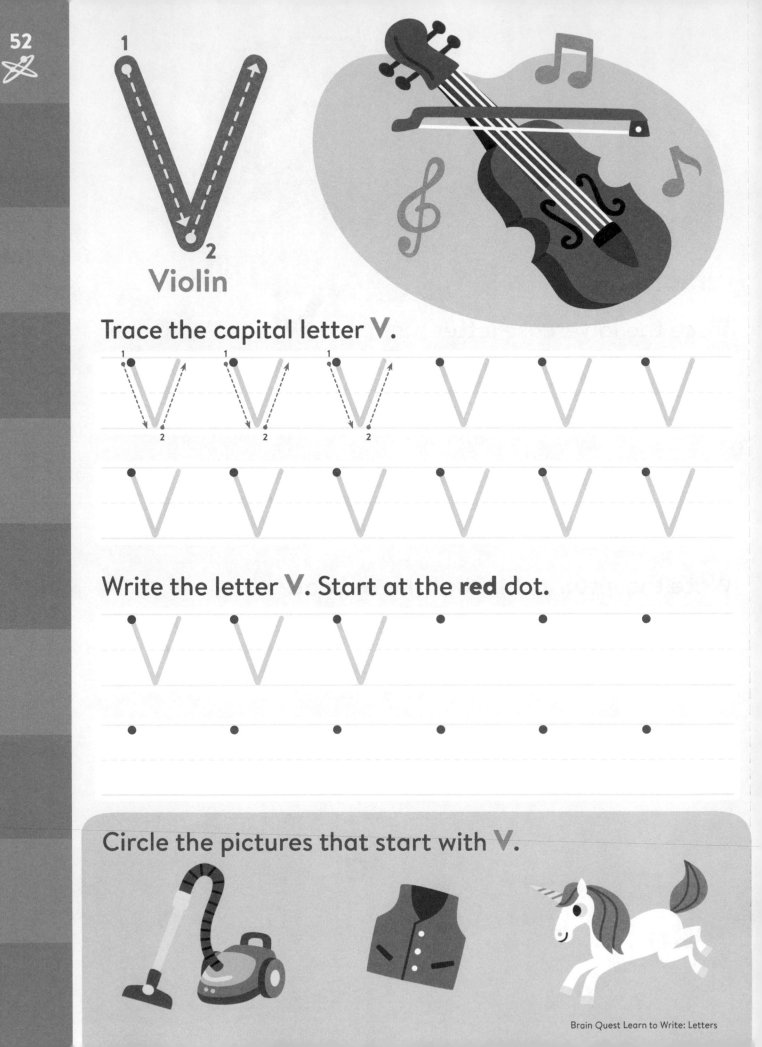

V

1

2

volcano

Trace the lowercase letter v.

v v v v v v

v v v v v v

Write the letter v. Start at the red dot.

v v v

Trace the v.

van

PLACE STICKER HERE

W

1 **3**

2 **4**

Watermelon

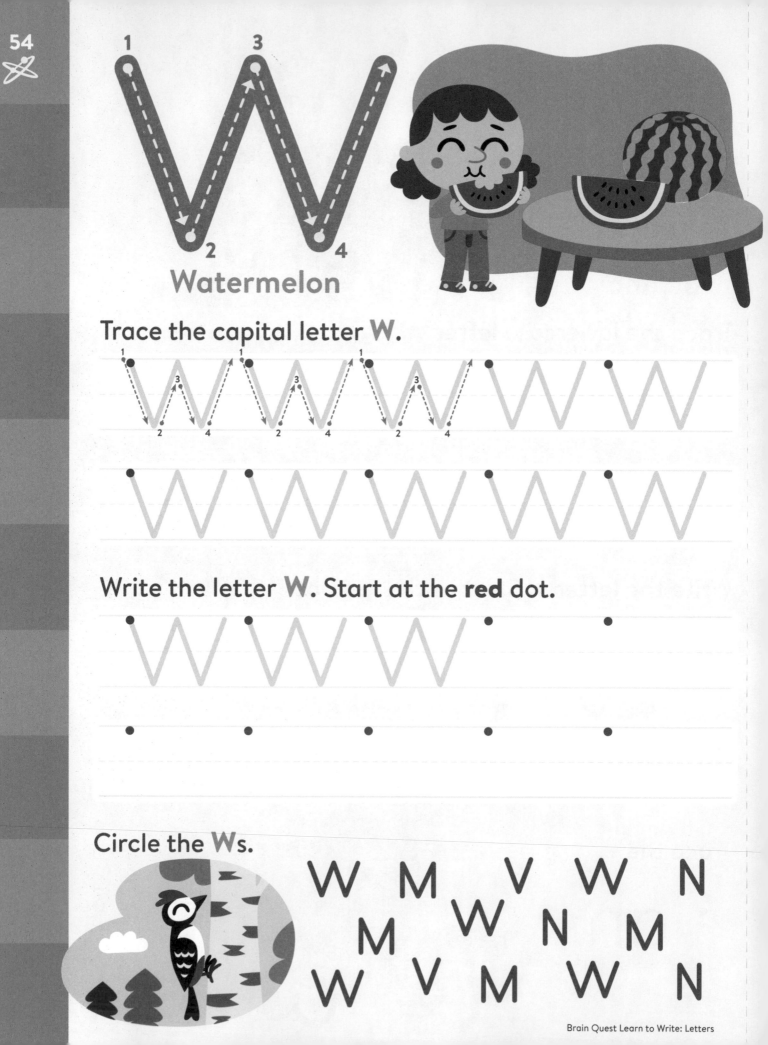

Trace the capital letter W.

W W W W W

W W W W W

Write the letter W. Start at the red dot.

W W W

Circle the Ws.

W M V W N

M W N M

W V M W N

W
woodwinds

Trace the lowercase letter w.

w w w w w w

w w w w w w

Write the letter w. Start at the red dot.

w w w

Write the missing w.

aterfall

PLACE STICKER HERE

1 2

Xylophone

Trace the capital letter X.

X X X X X X

X X X X X X

Write the letter X. Start at the red dot.

X X X

Trace the X.

X-ray

1 **2**
X

fox

Trace the lowercase letter x.

X X X X X X

X X X X X X

Write the letter x. Start at the red dot.

X X X

Trace the xs.

six boxes

PLACE STICKER HERE

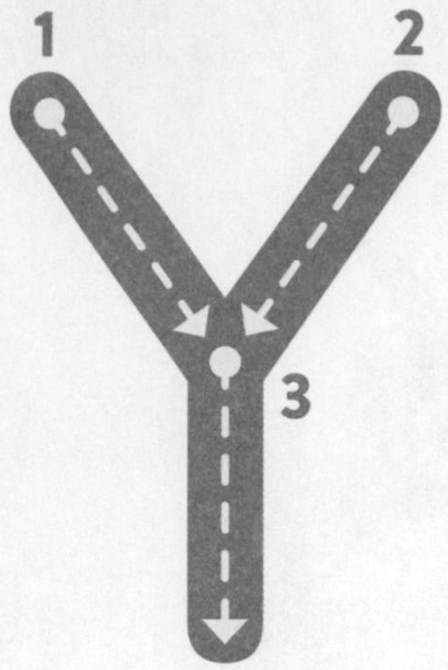

Yak

Trace the capital letter Y.

Write the letter Y. Start at the red dot.

Circle each Y.

V Y A V A V A

Y V Y A V Y

y yellow

Trace the lowercase letter **y**.

Write the letter **y**.
Start at the **red** dot.

Trace the **y**s.

yo-yo

Z Z

Zebra

Trace the capital letter Z.

Write the letter Z. Start at the **red** dot.

Trace the Z.

Zero

z

ZOO

Trace the lowercase letter **z**.

Write the letter **z**. Start at the **red** dot.

Trace the **z**.

zipper

PLACE STICKER HERE

Let's Review

Trace the letters in
the labels.

Stork

Quetzal

Robin

Toucan

Trace the words.
Match each word to a picture.

Woodwinds

Violin

Ukulele

Yak

Zebra

A to Z

Trace the capital letters from **A** to **Z**.

A B C

D E F G

H I J K L

M N O P Q

R S T U V

W X

Y Z

a to z

Trace the lowercase letters from **a** to **z**.

a b c d

e f g

h i j k l

m n o p q

r s t u

v w x

y z

Letter Matching

Match the capital and lowercase letters.

S   m

M

Y   x

A   a

B   r

X   i

I   s

R   y

L   b

l

Patterns

Look at the letters. Do you see a pattern?
Write the letter that comes next.

A a A a A a A a

b B b B b B b B

C D C D C D C D

e f e f e f e f

So Many Ss!

Draw a line from the letter S to the words that start with S.

Face Trace

Point to each part of the face.
Say the word out loud.
Trace the letters in each word.

hair

forehead

eye

nose

ear

mouth

cheek

teeth

Get Dressed

Point to each item of clothing.
Say the word out loud.
Trace the letters in each word.

hat

coat

mittens

pants

umbrella

boots

B for Bee

Circle all the **b**s.

d a h d
b b d b h
a h a a
d b d h a

Draw a line from the big **b** to the words that start with **b**.

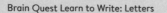

Animal Map

What places are on the map?
Trace the words.
Color in the animals!

jungle

forest

waterfall

farm

pond

zoo

island

Animal Babies

Say the name of each baby animal.
Trace its name.
Then write its name on the lines.

cub

puppy

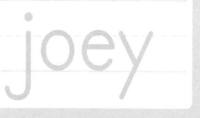

joey

kitten

Fruit Fun

Say the name of each fruit.
Trace its name.
Then write its name on the lines.

apple

peach

lemon

orange

lime

Color Names

Trace each color's name.
Then write the color's name.

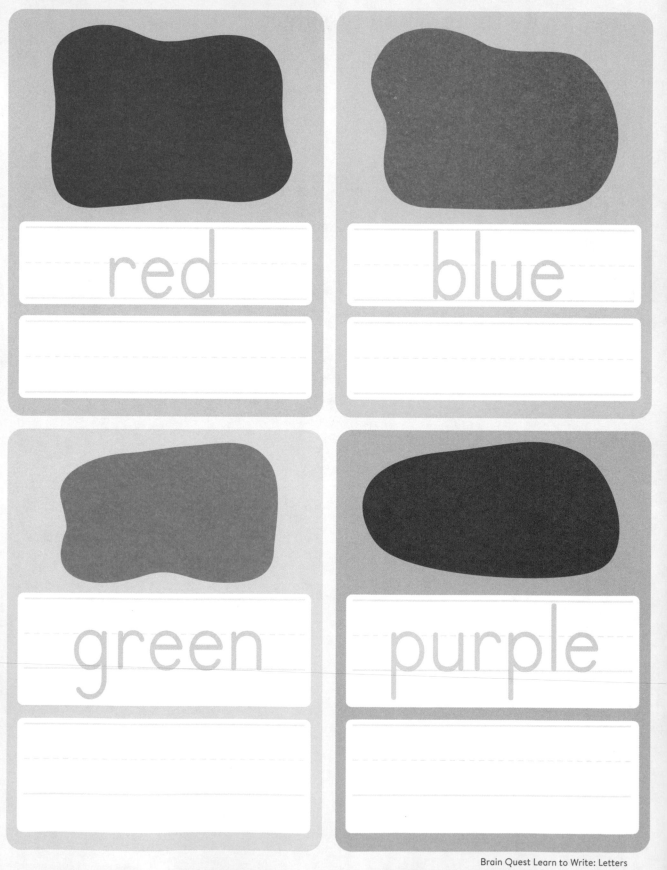

red

blue

green

purple

Take Shape

Trace each shape's name.
Then write the shape's name.

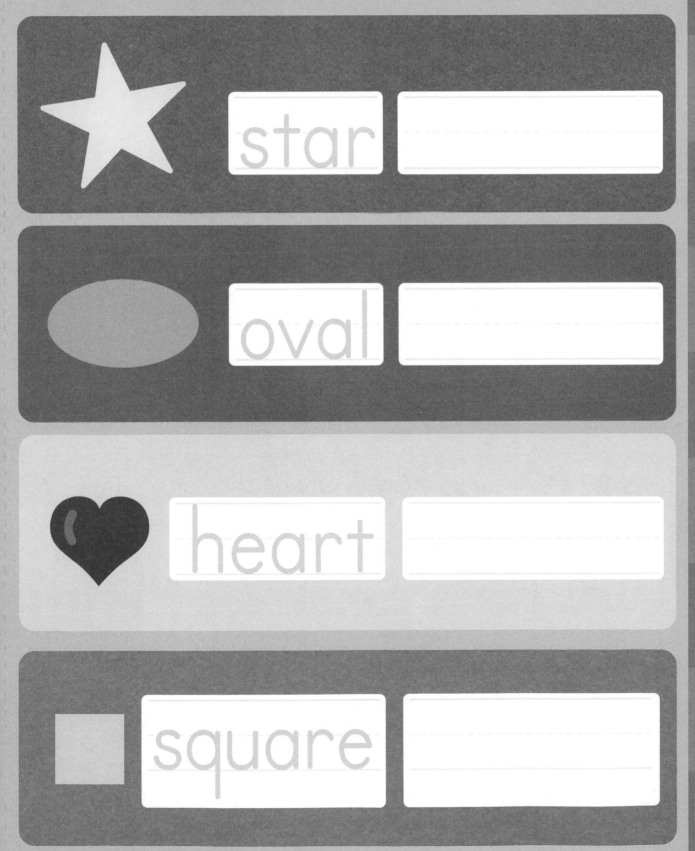

star

oval

heart

square

My Name Is

Practice writing your first name on the lines below.

Practice writing your last name on the lines below.

CONGRATULATIONS!

Write your name here:

COMPLETED

LEARN to WRiTE LETTERS

PLACE STICKER HERE

THERE'S MORE LEARN to WRiTE

Practice tracing and writing lines, shapes, and numbers with

More from America's #1 Educational Bestseller

BRAIN QUEST

Available wherever books are sold, or visit **brainquest.com.**

workman

Trace the letters and color the stickers!